The Human Brain

Larry Kettelkamp

ENSLOW PUBLISHERS, INC.

Bloy St. & Ramsey Ave.   P.O. Box 38
Box 777   Aldershot
Hillside, N.J. 07205   Hants GU12 6BP
U.S.A.   U.K.

Library of Congress Cataloging in Publication Data

Kettelkamp, Larry.
    The human brain.

    Includes bibliography and index.
    Summary: Describes the anatomy and operations of the brain and aspects such as memory, biofeedback, and brain surgery.
    1. Brain —Juvenile literature. [1. Brain] I. Title. [DNLM: 1. Brain —anatomy & histology —popular works. 2. Brain — physiology —popular works. WL 300 K26h]
QP376.K395   1986   612'.82   86 –4417
ISBN 0-89490-126-5

Printed in the United States of America

10 9 8 7 6 5 4 3 2 1

Permission for picture reprint or adaptation is gratefully acknowledged as follows:

p. 47, from *The Integrated Mind,* by M.S. Gazzaniga and J.E. LeDoux, Plenum Press, 1978; p. 49, from *Left Brain, Right Brain,* by Sally P. Springer and Georg Deutsch, W.H. Freeman & Co., 1981; p. 51, from *Drawing on the Right Side of the Brain,* by Betty Edwards, J.P. Tarcher Inc., 1979; p. 77, courtesy Siemens Medical Systems, Inc., 1985; pp. 78, 79, NMR scans, courtesy General Electric Co., 1985; p. 81, PET scans, courtesy Michael Phelps, UCLA School of Medicine, 1985.

With additional drawings by the author.

ACKNOWLEDGMENT

The author wishes to thank Marilyn Schmidt, pharmacologist, for offering critical suggestions. Thanks also is extended to those faculty members of the Rutgers Medical School who expressed helpful interest in the illustrations, and to the following people and sources for contributing materials and photographs: David Andrews, Oxford Superconductors; Michael Phelps, U.C.L.A. School of Medicine; General Electric Co.; and Siemens Medical Systems, Inc.

CONTENTS

FOREWORD

The brain is the command center of the human body. Its contents and connections determine personality, feelings, ideas, perceptions, and movement. When this important organ is damaged, people suffer from paralysis, incoordination, loss of the ability to speak, or the emotional and behavioral symptoms of mental illness.

The study of the human brain has produced an explosion of knowledge during the past ten to twenty years. Scientists now know much more than ever before about how this important organ works. *The Human Brain*, by Larry Kettelkamp, provides a good survey, expressed in simple language, of this exciting explosion of knowledge about the brain. In a clear, comprehensive manner, it provides readers with fundamental knowledge about the workings of the most important organ in their bodies.

Nancy C. Andreasen, M.D., Ph.D.
Professor of Psychiatry
The University of Iowa

1
MESSENGERS of BRAIN aNd Body

The Brain

The human brain resembles a bunch of cauliflower with a thick hairy rope hanging down underneath. This strange apparatus is the seat of thoughts and dreams, a computer that collects and processes information, and a storage bank for a lifetime of memories. It is a marvelous control center that runs the complicated machinery of the body. It is the site of emotions such as joy and anger and the creator of fantasies, music, art, science, and space-age inventions. It is the tool of the consciousness we call the mind.

This human brain is vastly complex, as is the nervous system that extends from it to communicate with all parts of the body. Yet the parts of the brain and nervous system are similar to those throughout the animal kingdom.

The simplest nervous systems are found in tiny organisms made of only a few cells. In these primitive organisms reactions to sunlight or pressure go directly from the surface to the

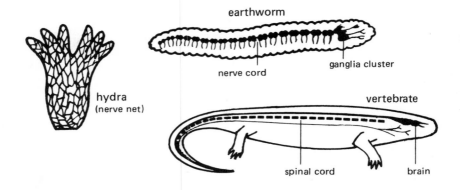

earthworm

ganglia cluster

nerve cord

hydra
(nerve net)

vertebrate

spinal cord

brain

inside. More advanced animals such as the hydra, a relative of the jellyfish, have a loose net of nerve cells. Anything that excites the hydra—a touch or a push—stimulates the whole nerve network.

In mollusks like the snail some nerve cells are grouped together to make control centers called ganglia. And in segmented worms such as the earthworm, the ganglia and the sense organs are clustered at one end to form a primitive head. Vertebrates are more developed, with a brain, spinal cord, and nerves reaching out and back from all parts of the body. The vertebrate brain is encased in a bony skull, and the spinal cord is covered by a series of bony cases.

In lower vertebrates such as the frog, brain parts grow in a simple row. In higher vertebrates this row is folded over and special parts are larger. In the mammals, those animals that provide milk for their young, the important part called the cerebrum covers the rest of the brain. The name *cerebrum* comes from the Latin word meaning "brain." In humans this section is folded back on itself to save space, and the entire brain surface, or cortex, is quite large in proportion to body weight and size. The brains of elephants and whales are huge, though the cortex is proportionally smaller than that of a human. Dolphins have brains larger than humans, with

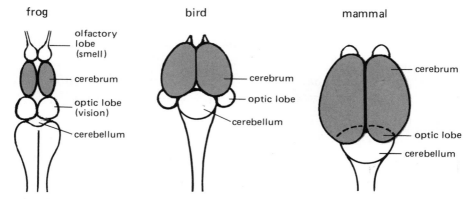

frog   bird   mammal

olfactory lobe (smell)
cerebrum
optic lobe (vision)
cerebellum

cerebrum
optic lobe
cerebellum

cerebrum
optic lobe
cerebellum

Comparing relative proportions of brain parts. Highest brain center, the cerebrum, (grey area) is smallest in frog, larger in bird, and largest in mammal.

more folds in the cerebrum. Dolphins possess exceptional intelligence, and their brains are highly specialized. For example, a dolphin can make stereo sounds through air holes in the right and left sides of the head. And a dolphin can carry on more than one conversation at a time by producing sounds of different frequencies, like the separate channels of radio broadcasts.

(To learn the divisions of the human brain, it helps to look at the parts from the bottom up. First, a thickened section called the brainstem pushes up from the top of the spinal cord. This is the passageway that links messages going to and from the brain with the rest of the body. A swollen section of the brainstem is called the medulla, meaning "marrow," because it resembles the marrow inside a bone. Just above this is a thicker bulge called the pons, whose name means "bridge." It connects the medulla to the more developed brain regions still higher above.)

The medulla and the pons together are called the hindbrain. The hindbrain is the most primitive part of the brain, and attached behind it is a unit of folded tissue called the cerebellum, meaning, literally, "small brain." The pons and the medulla or brainstem not only route messages to and from the spinal cord but also help regulate breathing and heart rhythms. The bulging cerebellum handles information about positions of the body and the arms and legs. It also stores patterns of learned muscle movements that have become habits.

The top of the brainstem is designated the midbrain, and just above it are the thalamus and hypothalamus. In Greek, *thalamus* means "inside chamber," and *hypo* means "under." Indeed, the hypothalamus is a tiny section beneath the thalamus, which itself is buried inside the skull and covered by the rest of the brain. This compact middle section is a relay station and screening center for most of the information going to or from the higher brain centers.

The outer section of the human brain is by far the largest area. This is the forebrain, the most important part. It is named the cerebrum, meaning "brain" in Latin, and its outer layer is called the cerebral cortex. *Cortex* means "shell" or "rind." The cortex is packed inside the bony skull from front to back and from side to side and is protected by membranes and fluids. The cerebral cortex is covered with deep grooves, which actually are folds. Besides the smaller tucks and folds, the whole cortex is folded up underneath itself like a thick blanket so that it is really about three times as large as it seems from the outside.

Especially deep folds divide the cortex into lobes, or sections, named for their functions or their positions in the skull. The occipital lobe is at the back and integrates nerve signals from the eyes. On either side are the temporal lobes, used in hearing and speech. Above and just behind these sections are the parietal lobes, involved in sensory responses and muscle control. Across the forehead are the frontal lobes, which consolidate information from the other lobes of the cortex.

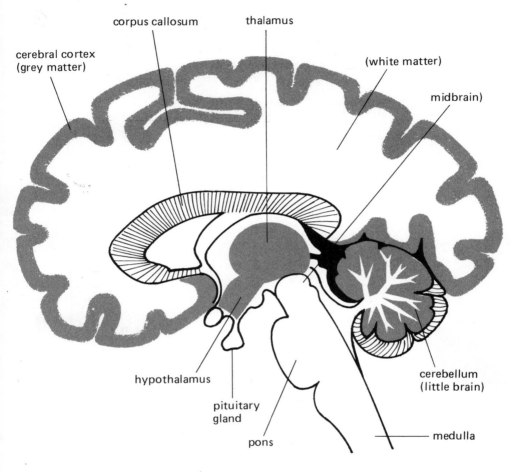

corpus callosum   thalamus

cerebral cortex
(grey matter)

(white matter)

midbrain)

hypothalamus

pituitary
gland

pons

cerebellum
(little brain)

medulla

Vertical cross section of the human brain showing important sections and parts.

   The cortex of the brain actually has developed as two complete sections or hemispheres, each resembling half a ball or sphere. And on each hemisphere between the large frontal lobes and the parietal lobes are narrow strips of folded cortex that are highly important.

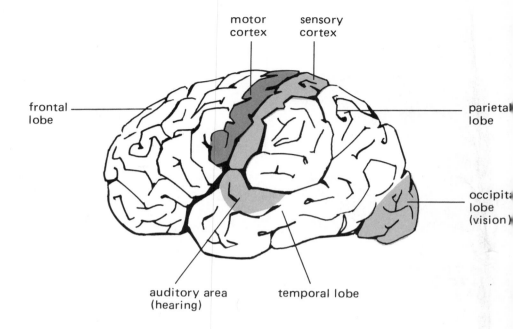

motor   sensory
cortex   cortex

frontal   parietal
lobe   lobe

                                                                occipital
                                                                lobe
                                                                (vision)

auditory area   temporal lobe
(hearing)

First are the motor strips, or motor cortex, responsible for commands for movement that go to various parts of the body. Parallel with the motor strips and behind them are the strips called the sensory cortex. These coordinate all information coming from the senses.

Inside the cerebral hemispheres is a package of brain parts called the limbic system. *Limbic* means "border," and this section follows the curved inside borders of the cortex. Many parts are nested into this space. There are two of each, and they are named for their unusual shapes. For instance, *amygdala* means "almond," and this part is shaped like a nut. Curving away behind this like the letter *s* is the hippocampus, whose name means "sea horse." Another part called the basal ganglion, or "nerve knot," consists of a lentiform—"lens-shaped"—ball which curves out into a tail called the caudate nucleus.

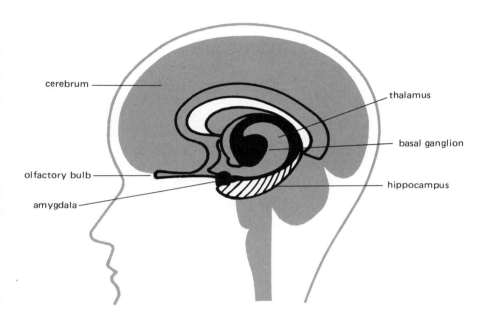

cerebrum

thalamus

basal ganglion

olfactory bulb

hippocampus

amygdala

Limbic system follows inner "limb," or curve, of the cerebral cortex. These inner brain parts are involved in memory and emotion. The olfactory bulb, or smell sensor, is linked to these structures. The basal ganglia (not part of the limbic system) relay information about physical movements.

The basal ganglia handle relay signals for the body's muscle movements. The hippocampi help the brain to learn and to organize memories. And this whole cluster of inside brain parts is tucked over and around the thalamus. All of these small parts sit on top of the brainstem and are covered by the cerebral cortex as if by an umbrella.

Whatever their particular functions, these brain parts are all interconnected so that messages are routed in a complete network. The brain and its parts may look strange, but acting as a unit it is a marvelous and efficient organ. In the sections of this

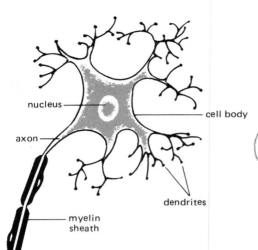

nucleus
cell body
axon
dendrites
myelin
sheath

Nerve cell, called a neuron, may be from a fraction of an inch to several feet long. Axon carries outgoing messages. Dendrites bring incoming messages. Fatty myelin sheath supplies electrical insulation.

book that follow, we will take a closer look at the workings of the human brain and its amazing communications systems.

Chemicals and Circuits

The brain is made up of living cells. The most important of these are the nerve cells, or neurons. Basically, a neuron resembles other cells found throughout the body. It has a cell wall called a plasma membrane. Inside the cell is sticky material called cytoplasm. This contains highly specialized parts. One part is the nucleus, which holds the twisted threads of deoxyribonucleic acid (DNA). DNA is the material that governs heredity. Genes located on these threads contain coded information that instructs the cell to manufacture certain proteins. These determine the type and function of the cell. Most body cells can divide so that the number of cells is multiplied, and old or dying cells are replaced. However, neurons cannot divide and multiply. Instead they grow extensions, much as a single tree grows limbs and branches throughout its life.

The neuron extensions are of two kinds. The first type is called the axon, meaning "axis" or "long line." Its job is sending out chemical messages to other neurons. The second type is called the dendrite, from a Greek word meaning "tree." Its job is to receive messages from other neurons. A neuron may have one or two axons and many dendrites or only a few, depending on its job and how much it is used. Both axons and dendrites may branch off into smaller extensions and fibers along their lengths. The axons or dendrites of a neuron may be as short as a few millimeters or as long as one meter in nerve cells that extend to outer parts of the body.

All body cells and parts are built of atoms. Each atom contains a certain number of particles called electrons. The electrons have charges of electricity that balance the positive charges also contained in each atom. Sometimes atoms lose or gain electrons. Such unbalanced, or charged, atoms are called ions. The cells of the human body tend to contain more negative than positive ions. Thus the cells have a slight and constant negative charge. This is also true of the nerve cells.

The cells of the body float in a liquid bath or plasma that fills the spaces between them. Liquid plasma, called cerebrospinal fluid, also is found inside the spinal column and in the otherwise empty spaces between the parts of the brain. This fluid is made up of various kinds of salty water, something like that found in the oceans. Within the fluid, atoms easily exchange electrons so the balance of negative and positive charges stays about equal.

The membrane that forms the wall of a body cell is semipermeable, which means that under certain conditions some of the salts in the body fluid can permeate, or penetrate, the cell membrane. A salt may pass either from outside to inside or from inside to outside. However, some salts, such as potassium, normally can enter the cell from the plasma much more easily than others, such as sodium or calcium.

It happens that the fluid surrounding the cells contains a great deal of sodium and not much potassium. However, inside the cells it is just the reverse. There is lots of potassium and not much sodium. Ions of sodium carry a positive electrical charge.

Ions of potassium also carry a positive electrical charge. However, the total electrical charge of all chemicals within the cell is still negative compared with the surrounding fluid.

Neurons take advantage of this natural imbalance in a special way. Certain stimuli can change the properties of the cell membrane temporarily. When this happens, sodium ions can enter the cell much more easily than usual. As sodium ions rush in through the cell wall, they force out potassium ions. But these move more slowly, and for less than one-thousandth of a second the cell becomes positively charged.

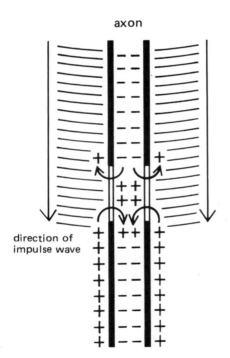

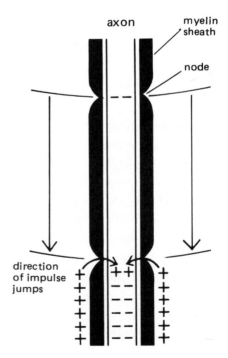

Neuron normally has negative (−) charge inside. When it is stimulated, sodium ions (+) temporarily flow through cell membrane. Positive charge is passed from one area to the next as a nerve impulse.

Some longer neurons are insulated by sections of myelin sheath. Nerve impulse then jumps directly between gaps, or nodes. Nerve impulses may travel up to 1000 miles per hour.

The cell quickly corrects this situation, and the cell membrane returns to its usual condition of allowing more potassium ions than sodium ions to enter. However, the brief electrical imbalance starts a chain reaction that moves along the nerve cell, starting with the dendrite that has been activated at its receiving end. The electrical reversal moves along the cell from one part to the next to create a ripple, or wave. This electrical wave pulse carries the information between neurons in the brain and those leading to and from skin, muscles, and various body organs.

Nerve fibers, both the axons and the dendrites, are reinforced by long inside stringers called microtubules. These add structural support. Another function of the microtubules is to help transfer chemicals on their surfaces. Thus materials synthesized in the nucleus move along each axon to a tiny bulb-shaped bulge in the end. The bulb contains tiny sacs that hold a chemical called a neurotransmitter. When a nerve impulse arrives at the end of the axon, it stimulates the sacs to fuse with the outer cell membrane. Their chemical then is released into the space between the axon and a neighbor neuron. This minute space between one neuron and the next is called a synapse, meaning "connection" in Greek.

Suppose an axon releases its chemical transmitter. This transmitter then crosses the gap to a dendrite, the receiving fiber of the neighbor neuron. The neurotransmitters cause channels to open at one or more receptor sites in the cell membrane of the dendrite. This allows positive sodium ions to enter and positive potassium ions to be released. The dendrite becomes unbalanced and sends an electrical pulse to its cell nucleus. Following this action the neurotransmitter is reabsorbed by the axon and returned to the storage sacs. Even though one neuron does not quite touch the next, the chemicals in the synaptic gap pass the message on down the line. There are many different types of neurotransmitter chemicals. More than fifty already have been discovered, each with a somewhat different job to do. All of them work by triggering neurons to fire electrically.

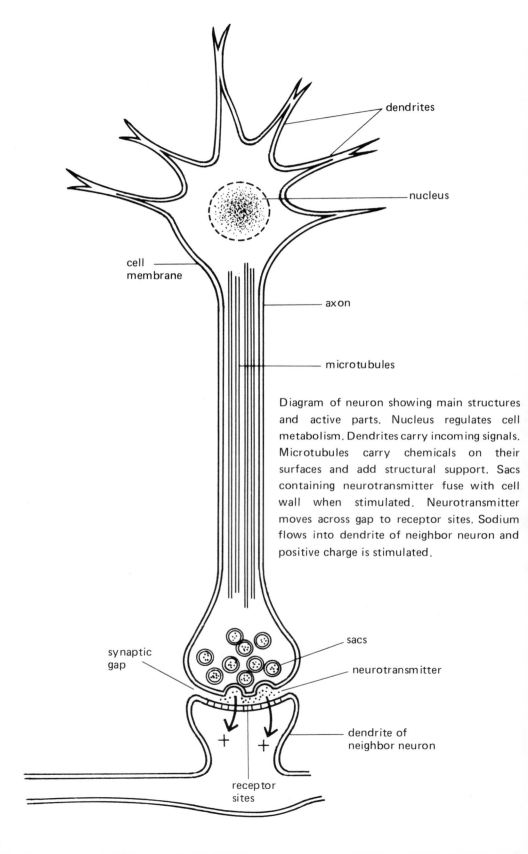

dendrites

nucleus

cell
membrane

axon

microtubules

Diagram of neuron showing main structures
and active parts. Nucleus regulates cell
metabolism. Dendrites carry incoming signals.
Microtubules carry chemicals on their
surfaces and add structural support. Sacs
containing neurotransmitter fuse with cell
wall when stimulated. Neurotransmitter
moves across gap to receptor sites. Sodium
flows into dendrite of neighbor neuron and
positive charge is stimulated.

sacs

synaptic
gap

neurotransmitter

dendrite of
neighbor neuron

receptor
sites

In addition to an electrical command for a neighbor neuron to fire, a command also can be sent *not* to fire. In this case the neurotransmitter released at the synapse allows negatively charged salts, such as chloride ions, to enter the receiving cell rather than positively charged sodium. The inside of the receiving cell is already negative, so this exchange keeps things as they are and prevents the neighbor cell from firing.

Neurons are different in size as well as in the length and number of their extensions—the axons and dendrites. They can interconnect in an almost endless variety of combinations. Some neurons are local, making connections with only a few close neighbor neurons. Other neurons reach out to interconnect with a great many target neurons. Such a neuron can send messages in many directions and also can receive a large number of input signals from the many neurons it is linked with.

Spaces between nerve cells and their connections are packed with other cells. These cells are called glia, which means "glue," since they appear to hold or support the neurons. There are many times more glia cells than neurons, and they seem to have a number of important jobs. Some glia cells apparently are busy cleaning up excess chemicals from the transfers at the synapses and along the nerve fibers. Some may help direct the flow of blood and oxygen to needed areas while others act as scavengers to get rid of pieces of damaged neurons. Still others may contribute to the chemical exchanges between neurons.

One important kind of glia cell is the oligodendrocyte. Its job is to form a material called myelin, which wraps around some nerve fibers to insulate them. This insulation works the same way as the wrapping around an electric wire. It shields the electrical activity within the nerve from outside influences and helps the messenger signal to travel more efficiently.

The Nervous System

The brain and spinal cord are a basic working unit. In all of the higher animals, including humans, there are bony casings to protect this unit from damage. The bones of the skull, or cranium, close almost completely around the brain, and a series of small bones called vertebrae, supported by cushions called discs, surround the spinal cord to protect it from injury.

Within the vertebrae the spinal cord is shielded by the same membranes and fluid that also surround the brain. The fluid protects the brain and spinal cord from shock. The outermost layer of the spinal cord is a whitish color and consists of insulated nerve fibers that carry messages both up and down the cord. This layer is called the white matter. Hidden inside the cord are columns of grey matter forming an elongated unit that resembles a steel girder. If the cord is sliced across, the grey matter looks something like a pair of open butterfly wings.

The grey matter contains nerve fibers that transmit signals both into and out of the cord. Bundles of nerve fibers called spinal nerves leave the spinal column through holes in the vertebrae. Those that lead out toward the front of the body carry messages to the muscles, signaling them to contract and cause the body to move. Those fibers leading out toward the back of the body bring incoming signals from the body's surface as well as from muscles and other body parts. In addition, a bulge along the edge of each "butterfly wing" holds nerves belonging to a special network called the autonomic nervous system.

In all, there are thirty-one pairs of nerves leading out from the spinal cord at either side. These spinal nerves are divided into four groups. Nerves at the top of the column beneath the head are called cervical, meaning "neck." They go to the throat, chest, arms, and hands. The next and largest group of spinal nerves is called thoracic, meaning "chest" or "breastplate." These nerves reach out to all the parts of the body from the collar to the lower ribs and stomach. The third group of nerves is called lumbar, meaning "girdle" or "loins." These nerves go to the front parts of the legs and feet and the sex organs. And the last group of nerves is called sacral because the last five vertebrae are fused together to form the sacrum, and this bone was once thought to be sacred. The sacral nerves lead to the back parts of the legs and the soles of the feet.

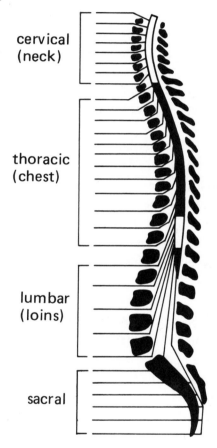

cervical
(neck)

thoracic
(chest)

lumbar
(loins)

sacral

Main groups of spinal nerves. Cervical nerves reach throat, chest, arms and legs. Thoracic nerves reach mid-body from collarbone to lower ribs. Lumbar nerves reach front of legs and feet. Sacral nerves reach back of legs and soles of feet.

Together the brain and spinal cord form the body's main control unit, called the central nervous system, or CNS. Its job is to receive all of the incoming sensory information, sort it, process it, and make decisions. Normally the brain analyzes the information. Then it sends commands for muscle movements down the spinal column, which routes them through outgoing nerve fibers to the correct body sections. But sometimes in an emergency there is no time to get the information to the brain and wait for a decision. For example, suppose you accidentally touch a hot stove. In this case the sensory signals get only as far as the spinal column. A gap is bridged between a sensory neuron and a motor neuron, and signals are immediately sent to the muscles of your arm to withdraw. Your spinal column has made a quick decision. Of course the message is also relayed to your brain. You will sense pain and observe what has happened, and then you will decide what to do about it. For instance, you probably will choose not to touch the stove again, and you might decide to put your fingers in cool water to reduce the swelling and pain.

The nerve network leading from the spinal column to all parts of the body is called the peripheral nervous system, or PNS. *Periphera* means "outer border," and this nervous system does indeed stretch all the way to the tips of your fingers and toes and to the skin at the body surface.

The part of the PNS that helped you to pull your hand away from the hot stove and put your fingers in cool water carries the motor impulses of the body. It is called somatic, meaning "of the body." The other part, called sensory, handles signals coming into the brain from all the body's senses. There are special receptors at the back of your eyeballs, inside your ears, on the surface of your tongue and skin, and in your nostrils, muscles, and joints. These receptors bring the sensations of light, sound, odor and taste, pain, pressure, and balance that keep you constantly informed about what is happening around and to your body.

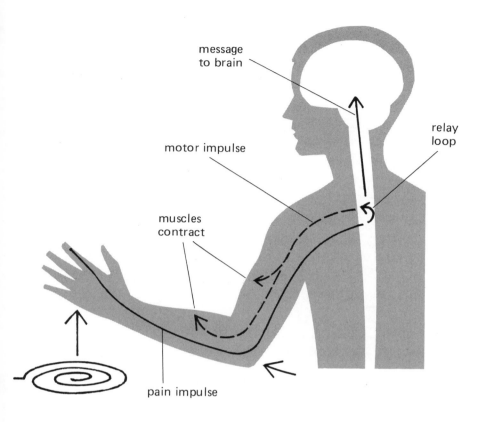

message to brain

relay loop

motor impulse

muscles contract

pain impulse

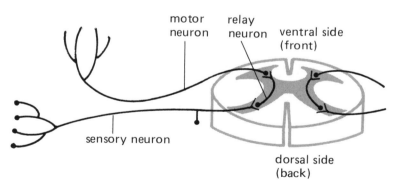

motor neuron

relay neuron

ventral side (front)

sensory neuron

dorsal side (back)

Reflex action. Finger touches hot stove. Pain receptor sends impulse to spinal column. Relay loop routes motor impulse directly to arm muscles, which contract to lift hand and arm. Pain message arrives later at brain. Cross section of spinal cord shows pairs of nerves leading out each side. Fibers at front (ventral) carry nerve impulses to muscles. Fibers at back (dorsal) bring incoming sensory signals.

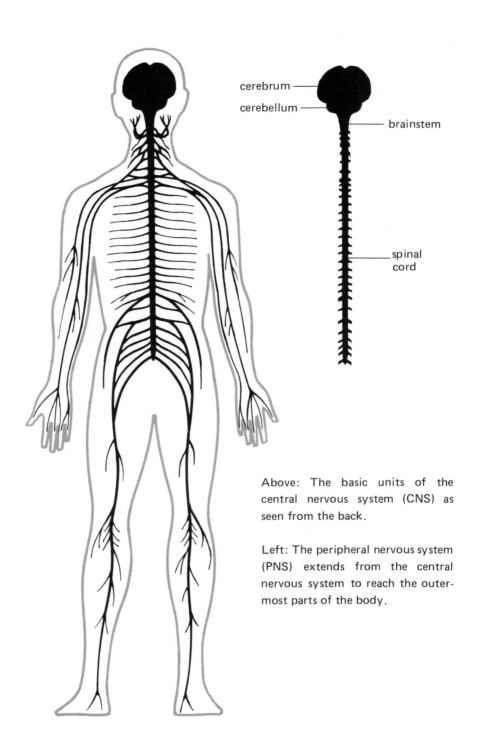

cerebrum

cerebellum

brainstem

spinal
cord

Above: The basic units of the
central nervous system (CNS) as
seen from the back.

Left: The peripheral nervous system
(PNS) extends from the central
nervous system to reach the outermost parts of the body.

The autonomic nervous system, or ANS, is a mysterious part of the network of nerve cells. *Auto* means "having its own separate rules," and this special portion of the nervous system does its work like a computer that has been programmed and then forgotten. Usually we are not consciously aware of the workings of the autonomic system. It regulates the body's inner activities—the flow of blood, heartbeat, breathing, muscular contractions of the stomach and intestines involved in digestion, and the activities of other organs such as the liver, pancreas, and kidneys.

One part of the ANS, called sympathetic, makes the heart beat faster, opens the pupils of the eyes wider, speeds breathing, activates the sweat glands, and routes more blood to the muscles and brain. This part automatically takes over whenever a person is excited or frightened. It is an emergency system that prepares the body for "fight or flight." With sympathetic action the nerves work as a unit.

The other part of the ANS is called parasympathetic, meaning "in addition to sympathetic." This part acts in just the opposite way. The nerves work individually to slow the heart to normal rate, contract the pupils of the eye, and direct blood to the stomach, intestines, and other internal organs to stimulate their normal functions. (Actually, the digestive system has its own special autonomic network as part of the PNS.) Thus the parasympathetic part of the ANS works automatically to keep the inner activities of the body "on track," neither overworking nor underworking. The two divisions of the autonomic nervous sytem tend to balance each other. They keep the body regulated like a fine machine, but able to react instantly to outside needs and stresses.

One subdivision of the nervous system is connected directly to the brain rather than routed through the spinal cord. The nerves are short and direct. They are called cranial nerves, and there are twelve pairs in all. These nerves connect directly to the

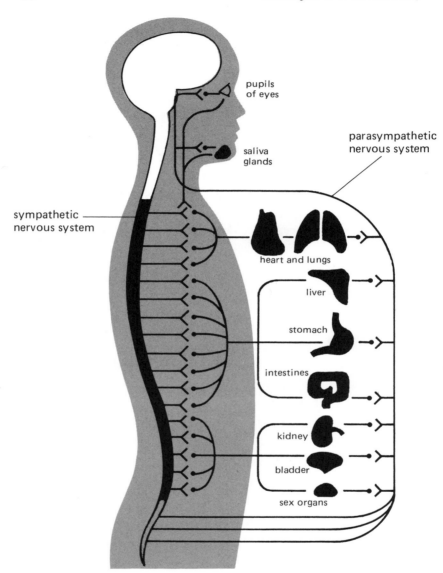

pupils
of eyes

parasympathetic
nervous system

saliva
glands

sympathetic
nervous system

heart and lungs

liver

stomach

intestines

kidney

bladder

sex organs

Simplified schematic showing divisions of the autonomic nervous system and some of the internal organs they serve. Sympathetic system activates body for emergency. Parasympathetic system stimulates regular normal functions.

eyes, ears, and nose to transmit incoming sensory signals. Other cranial nerves go to the muscles that move each eyeball. Still others are involved in sensations and movements of muscles in the face and sensations and movements in the throat and tongue, the shoulders, and even the heart and the organs in the abdomen.

It is estimated that the brain and nervous systems of the human body contain as many as fifty billion neurons, each connected to from one hundred to ten thousand other neurons. And all of these cells are able to coordinate their activities as a working unit within this huge control-and-communications system.

2
Sensing and Acting

The Senses

The brain cannot function without the special communications signals that come from the various bodily sense organs, which provide information about sight, sound, smell, taste, touch, and balance. In a way, these highly developed systems and organs are extensions of the brain itself.

The human eye works like a camera. A lens at the front of the eyeball focuses an upside-down image on the retina at the back. The retina is a layer of nervous tissue consisting of specialized cells. Cells called cones are clustered near the middle of the retina and are sensitive to bright daylight. The cones also are sensitive to particular light frequencies, that is, to colors. Apparently, colors are sensed and coded for the brain in combinations of red with green and of yellow with blue. Other cells called rods are mostly scattered toward the edges of the retina. These cells are extremely sensitive only to brightness. Their action predominates at night, when color seems to disappear. In total, the retina of each eye contains about 100 million rods and cones.

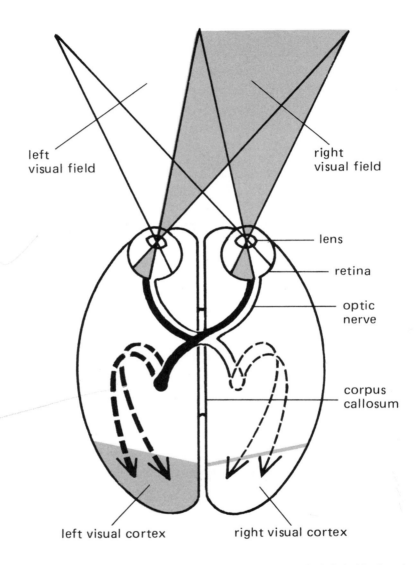

Information from right visual field falls on receptors in left half of each eye and is passed by nerve bundles to left hemisphere. Information from left visual field falls on receptors in right half of each eye and is passed to right hemisphere.

Information collected by additional layers of cells in each eye is signaled to the brain through a nerve bundle called the optic nerve. The two optic nerves meet in the center of the brain, where about half of the fibers in each cross to the other side. Therefore, some signals cross and are passed to the opposite side of the brain, while other signals remain on the same side as the eye. So when both eyes are used, information from the left half of the visual field is processed by the right side of the brain and vice versa. Visual signals first reach a tiny unit called the geniculate body and then arrive at the visual cortex at the back of the brain on either side of the head. There the brain responds as if the enlarged details of the retinal image were laid out within the brain itself.

Various layers of brain cells detect changes in the brightness of light as points, fringes or surrounds, edges, and bars, even sensing changing angles and directions. Apparently, the spacings of the patterns are mathematically simplified by the brain to create a complete "readout" organized something like a computer image.

In addition, each eye sees a slightly different view of the world. The information, along with the image detail, is combined and processed in higher brain centers at the sides and front of the brain to give a complete understanding of the space that surrounds us. Indeed, more than a dozen vision centers of the brain involve almost two-thirds of the cortex in this complex process.

The human ear is sensitive to sounds in a range of vibrations between about 20 and 20,000 pulses per second. Vibrating objects create pressure waves that travel through the air. These sound waves are gathered by the ear, where a membrane called the eardrum vibrates sympathetically. Through tiny bones connected to a second membrane these vibrations are magnified and carried to the fluid within a tiny coiled passage called the cochlea, meaning "snail." A tapered membrane runs the length of the cochlea and vibrates in response to high or low frequencies according to its proportions and position along the curves of the organ.

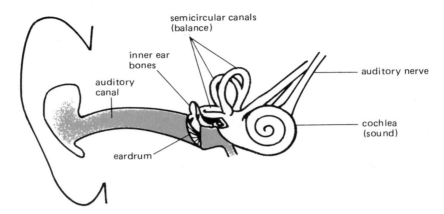

Sound pressure waves enter auditory canal and excite eardrum. Small bones transfer vibrations to fluid inside cochlea. Semicircular canals detect changes in body posture.

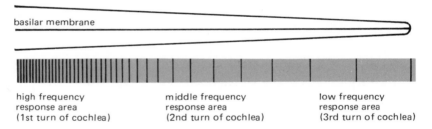

high frequency   middle frequency   low frequency
response area   response area   response area
(1st turn of cochlea)   (2nd turn of cochlea)   (3rd turn of cochlea)

Cross section of cochlea. Hairlike receptors in basilar membrane respond to sound vibrations according to their location.

Minute hair cells along the membrane sense these vibrations and transmit complex information to the brain through the a-coustic nerve. The two acoustic nerves, one for each ear, meet at the brainstem, where, as with the eyes, some signals cross over to opposite sides of the brain, while others remain on the same side with each ear. Sound sensations are processed chiefly in the temporal lobes at the sides of the brain. Much as the two eyes create stereo or depth vision, the ears receive sounds in stereo, and the brain interprets the differences in timing of the signals to compute the head's left-and-right position within the space around it.

Smell and taste are related because with each, tiny nerve organs called chemoreceptors identify substances just by touching some of their molecules suspended in saliva or mucous fluid. The chemoreceptors in the nose are many times as sensitive as those in the tongue, so the sense of smell is more acute. Molecules suspended in the air passing through the nose adhere to the mucous lining and touch the receptor fibers in the roof of the nose. There at least seven basic molecule "shapes," or odors, are apparently detected. Signals are transferred to a small olfactory bulb, above the bony covering on each side of the nose and from there to the brain's limbic system.

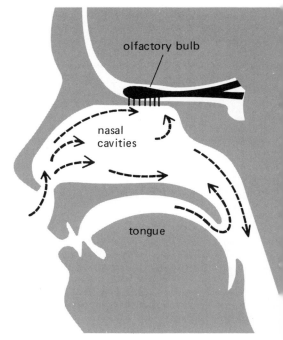

Inhaled air containing scent particles passes through nasal cavities. Aromatic particles from food in the mouth also circulate upwards. Some molecules are trapped and dissolved in mucous lining. Chemoreceptors from two olfactory bulbs above tops of nasal cavities identify substances by touch and send nerve signals to brain.

Similar chemical sensors are grouped across the surface of the tongue, especially at the sides and edges, in the tiny "pimples" that give the tongue its rough texture. Various areas of the tongue on each side from tip to back respond to the four sensations of salt, sweet, sour, and bitter. Taste sensations are routed to the brainstem, then to the thalamus and cerebral cortex. Most tastes are combinations of these four sensations.

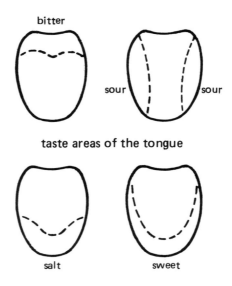

bitter

sour   sour

taste areas of the tongue

salt   sweet

Chemoreceptor cells in taste buds of the tongue detect dissolved substances. The front of the tongue is mainly sensitive to sweet and salt. The sides are sensitive to sour, and the back to bitter. Nerve impulses cross from each side of the tongue to opposite brain hemispheres.

Touch, pressure, and vibration are sensed by the body in several ways. Nerve endings near the skin of the body surface take the form of tiny bulbs, or clusters of minute fibers that wrap around body hairs. When these elements are pushed out of shape, nerve pulses are generated. Similar receptors report sensations from within the body, and still others relay information about the positions of joints and the stretching or contracting of muscles.

Among the pressure receptors are those that report pain. Gentle stimulation causes the sensation of itching. Greater pressure, particularly to small nerve fibers, causes sensations of pain, as does the bruising or cutting of cell tissues.

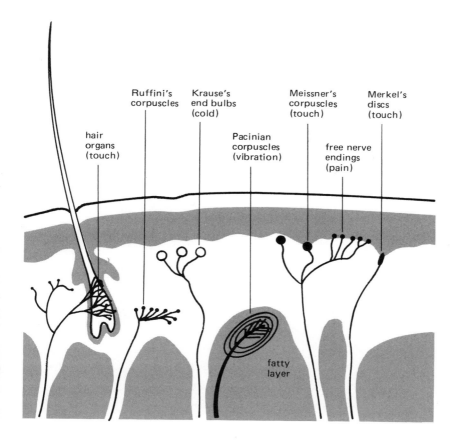

Cross section of skin and hair, showing nerve receptors sensitive to touch, pressure, pain, and temperature.

Nerve receptors sensitive to temperature seem divided into those that respond to heat and those that respond to cold, although not all functions are entirely clear. Apparently the brain can judge the temperature of the body surface by the balance between these signals and can take steps to keep the body comfortable.

The inner ear contains a system of vestibules, or chambers, filled with fluid. There are three loops, or semicircular canals, set at different angles to one another and the smaller chambers to which they are attached. When the head is moved or tilted, fluid sloshes through these organs. This causes tiny groups of hairs to bend in various directions, which in turn stimulates nerve signals to the brain. Sensations from the semicircular canals provide the brain with information on turning and tilting. Signals from the smaller chambers indicate the direction of the pull of gravity, enabling us to stand and balance the body even in complete darkness.

The Sensory Cortex

Between the frontal cortex and the parietal and temporal cortex are symmetrical strips running down either side of the brain. These strips are called the sensory cortex. They receive all the incoming signals from the body's senses: signals from the eyes and ears, signals of smell from the olfactory bulb, and signals of taste from the sensors in the tongue. Besides these there are signals coming in from the outer reaches of the body, including fine touch, pressure or vibration, heat, cold, and pain. Add to these the deep sensations of body position and muscle stretching as well as the inner ear's sense of balance and gravity, and the sensory cortex of the brain receives a constant supply of data about the world outside the body, the world within, and the relationship between the two.

The sensory cortex has specialized groups of neurons laid out in a sequence from the top of each strip to the bottom. In general this pattern matches parts of the body from the feet to the head. Large groups of neurons are allocated to the hands and face, since these are of great importance. Smaller groups of neurons are allocated for the other body parts. All of the incoming information is thus neatly collected and organized by the sensory cortex and routed to other areas of the cortex for analysis and decision making.

The Motor Cortex

The senses are closely coordinated with control of the muscular movements of the body. This relationship involves many parts of the brain and nervous system. Within the spinal network some nerves interact to make sure that as one muscle group contracts, an opposing group relaxes. In the brainstem other groups of neurons have the task of keeping the muscles "toned" so that they are neither too tight nor too loose. The basal ganglia near the thalamus act to make sure that all body movements are coordinated. And the cerebellum takes over the automatic control of fine muscle movements as they are learned and become habit.

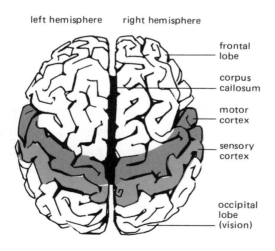

However, the chief brain area involved in overall control and planning of movements is the motor cortex. This area consists of matching strips on either side of the brain surface lying just in front of the sensory cortex.

To see how this control works, let's take an example. Suppose the frontal cortex has created a plan for swinging a baseball bat. There are several steps to the plan. A moving ball will be struck by using both arms to swing a bat through a particular arc. The body will be positioned over the back foot and will then shift over the front foot. Meanwhile, the trunk of the body will twist along with the motion of the arms. This plan is fed to the motor cortex. Instructions go out along separate motor pathways leading to the parts of the body to be activated. Other brain sections, including the cerebellum, which controls speed, timing, and smoothness, monitor the results as the plan is put into action.

Beginning in a fold of the motor strip at the top of the head are the neurons responsible for the foot, ankle, knee, hip, and trunk of the body. Following the curve of the motor strip down the side of the brain are cells linked to the shoulder, elbow, and wrist. The next segment, containing neurons for the hand and fingers, is enormously enlarged because of the fine muscle movements needed in those parts of the body. Next come the segments for neck, brow, eyes, face, lips, jaw, and tongue, also enlarged.

Motor cells on the left side of the brain control muscles on the right side of the body. Motor cells on the right side of the brain control muscles on the left side of the body. The result is balanced coordination between the symmetrical halves of the body.

The sensory cortex and motor cortex cooperate with the areas of higher judgment. This enables the brain to perceive and understand the world and the body to sit, stand, run, and perform all the complex tasks of human life.

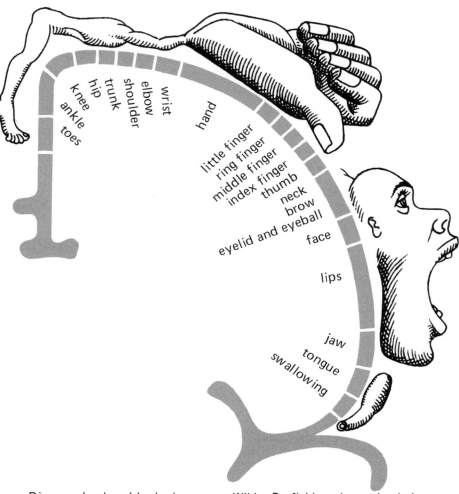

Diagram developed by brain surgeon Wilder Penfield to show stimulation points in brain's motor cortex that lead to muscle activity and position of body joints.

3

Right Brain, Left Brain

The Hemispheres

Many structures in the brain come in pairs. A unit on the left side matches a unit on the right like a mirror reflection. A top view of the cerebral cortex shows the most obvious division. The two halves of the cortex look something like the sliced halves of a melon that have not quite been put back together again. In fact, the two hemispheres are joined only deep within the brain by bundles of nerve fibers that form the corpus callosum, whose name means "hard body" (although it is not really hard).

The two halves of the brain look roughly the same, but their proportions may be somewhat different, depending on which brain areas are most developed on either side. Within the brainstem, bundles of nerve fibers from the right side of the body cross over to the left side of the brain, and nerves from the left side of the body cross over to the right side of the brain. As we already have seen, part of the nerve bundle from each eye also crosses over in the middle of the brain. Thus images that are in the left part of the visual field are processed on the right side of the brain, as are the nerve linkages to the muscles on the left side of the body. And the crossing pattern is reversed for the right side of the body and the left side of the brain.

However, not all brain functions are equally reflected between the hemispheres. The best example is speech and language. The first clues to the location of speech centers in the brain came from patients with brain damage. In the 1860s a French physician named Paul Broca had a patient who could read and write and could understand what was spoken to him. However, he had become unable to speak. This patient had sustained damage to a small section of the brain on the left side of the frontal lobe. Broca guessed correctly that this part was associated with speech, and so it was named Broca's area. In 1874 a brain surgeon named Carl Wernicke discovered a similar area on the left side of the head on the temporal lobe. Patients with damage to this area retained the ability to talk, but their speech made no sense. Somehow they had lost the ability to form logical sentences. This small brain section, called Wernicke's area, was also named after its discoverer.

Broca's area is in front of the part of the left motor cortex that controls signals sent to muscles of the face, jaw, tongue, and throat. Wernicke's area lies directly behind the left hemisphere section of the sensory cortex. Apparently, a language plan consisting of the form and meaning of words and sentences is transferred through nerve fibers from Wernicke's area to Broca's area. There it is coordinated into automatic commands to the muscles of the vocal cords, tongue, and lips through the motor cortex. Speech is the result.

In the human brain the areas that control speech and language are enlarged. Usually, but not always, these areas are found in the left hemisphere. The hemisphere that happens to control speech has some relationship to whether a person is right- or left-handed. Of all right-handers, ninety-five percent have speech control in the left hemisphere. Only about seventy percent of left-handers have speech control in the left hemisphere. Of the remaining thirty percent, half have speech control in the right hemisphere, and the other half have speech control divided between both hemispheres.

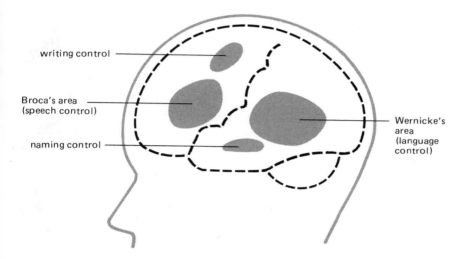

Analytical skills with words and numbers usually are controlled by the brain's left hemisphere. Areas associated with speech and language are named for their discoverers. Exact locations vary from person to person.

In an adult, damage to these important speech centers may be permanent. In the brain of a child who is still developing speech skills, however, damage to the speech side may stimulate the other hemisphere of the brain to take over speech in an entirely normal way. Although language skills seem to develop strongly in one side of the brain, the handling of motor skills, sensory skills, and other tasks seems more evenly divided between the hemispheres. Even so, these functions may work somewhat differently in each hemisphere. In many ways it is like having two brains instead of one.

The Split Brain

Sometimes, in very unusual situations, the connections between the hemispheres of the brain are cut. In a patient with epilepsy, brain waves that normally pulse separately may suddenly synchronize to generate an extra-large electrical charge that jolts the body into a fit or seizure. This can be very severe if the synchronized electrical pulses spill over from one hemisphere of the brain to the other. At one time, cutting the corpus callosum surgically to divide the hemispheres seemed the only way of treating such seizures.

Experiments with patients whose brains have been split apart in this way provide fascinating insights to the workings of the hemispheres. In most ways a split-brain patient may seem quite normal. He or she thinks, speaks, and goes about daily tasks with little difficulty. However, the right brain does not know what the left brain is thinking. Information from the language and speech areas on the left does not cross over to the right. And perceptions made by the right brain do not pass over to the left.

A device called a tachistoscope is used for experiments with split-brain patients. This machine flashes a picture onto a screen for a fraction of a second. Anyone looking at the screen sees the entire picture at a glance. In a split-brain experiment, the patient is seated directly in front of the blank screen and is asked to stare at a black dot in the middle of the screen. This aligns the patient's head with the screen so that when the picture flashes, everything to the left of the center line is perceived by the right brain and everything to the right of the center line is perceived by the left brain.

One such experiment was made by researchers Michael Gazzaniga and Joseph LeDoux with a male patient known as P.S. The picture flashed on the screen was divided into two parts. On the left was a snow scene with a house, an evergreen tree, and a snowman. On the right was a picture of a chicken's claw. Obviously, the two pictures had nothing to do with each other. Four cards with small pictures were placed near the left hand of P.S. and four more cards near his right hand. P.S. was asked to point to a picture on the left that seemed to go with the one he had seen flashed on the screen, and also to point to a card on the right that correlated with the picture flashed on the screen.

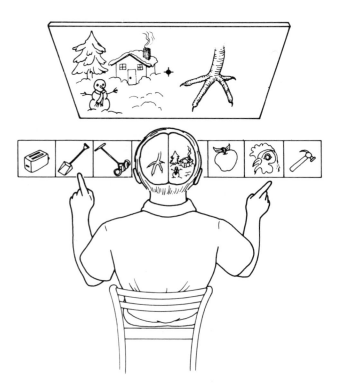

A split-brain patient views a dot in the middle of a screen. A picture is flashed on the screen briefly. The right brain sees and understands only the snow scene on the left. The left brain sees and understands only the chicken's claw on the right.

His left hand pointed to a snow shovel, and his right hand pointed to the head of a chicken. He was then asked, "What did you see?" P.S. answered, "I saw a claw and I picked the chicken, and you have to clean out the chicken shed with a shovel."

The patient's right hand was activated by the left brain, which saw a chicken's claw. His left hand was activated by the right brain, which saw the snow scene. The response of each brain hemisphere was correct. But to make sense of the whole picture, the patient had to invent a story that sounded logical and combined the shovel with the chicken. In this way the speech-controlling hemisphere of a split-brain patient tries to make a complete interpretation, even though the available information is incomplete.

Examples of how visual processing is divided between the hemispheres come from otherwise normal patients with damage at the back of the brain. If a patient has damage in the parietal or occipital lobe of the right hemisphere, there is sometimes a strange illness called neglect. The damaged area apparently cannot process information from the left visual field normally. So a neglect patient who is shaving might shave only the right half of his face. Or a neglect patient who is eating may take only the food from the right half of the plate, leaving that on the left untouched. Somehow the perception of space on the left is almost completely absent. If such a patient is asked to copy drawings of simple objects, part or all of the left half of each object may be missing.

Such clues from brain-damaged patients prove the independence of the brain's hemispheres and also suggest that the right side both perceives and processes information differently from the left. The left hemisphere works with words, details, counting, time, and sequences. It takes things apart in an analytical way. It has a narrow focus of attention. The right hemisphere sees shapes in space, joins parts into wholes, compares things, and sees relationships free of time. It handles ideas and images. It builds or synthesizes rather than analyzing. Of course, mental abilities vary widely from person to person. But it is interesting that on the average, men and boys show more ability with shapes in space, a right-brain function. And on the average, women and girls show more ability with language, which is usually a left-brain function.

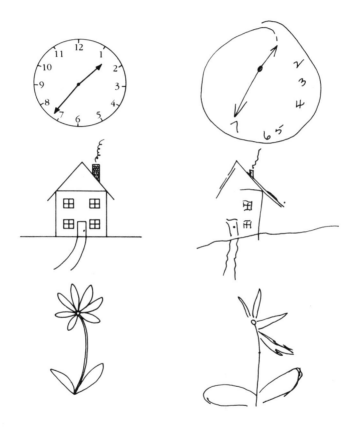

A neglect patient, with damage to the back of the brain on the right side, is asked to copy drawings of a clock, a house, and a flower. The patient's drawings leave out part of the left half of each picture as if it were not visible.

Artists and musicians use the capabilities of the right hemisphere. Those who believe they are not so artistic or creative may simply not be using this hemisphere actively. Let's suppose a person has strong ability in math and language and likes logical thinking but never has been able to draw well. One solution is to practice drawing upside down. A photograph to be copied is placed upside down next to a sheet of blank paper. In its upside-down position, the details of the photograph are hard to recognize. Instead, it looks like a jumble of lines and shapes. The analytical left brain has trouble deciphering the picture. But this is exactly what the right brain is best at—seeing related groups of shapes. And so in order to copy the picture at all, the right brain must be used to get the job done. People who thought they had no artistic ability have been amazed to find that talent suddenly appeared when the correct combination of brain hemisphere functions was stimulated.

The activities of the right brain are now thought to be of great importance. The right brain likes to play with images and ideas, bringing them together in new ways. But to test these ideas, the logical skills of the left brain must be brought into use. People who are both creative and practical, such as inventors, have learned to use the capabilities of the entire brain cooperatively. It is a matter of putting the unused parts to use.

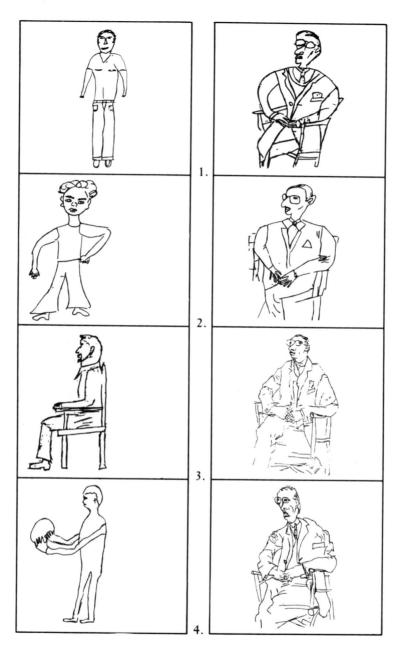

Left column: Drawings of people by four students show beginner's ability.

Right column: Same students copied a Picasso drawing. Students 1 and 2 copied drawing right side up. Details are clear but amateurish. Students 3 and 4 copied drawing upside down so details could not be recognized. Results show accurate proportion and perspective typical of right-brain perception.

4

Chemicals, States, and Moods

Glands and Emotions

One very important control unit in the brain is the hypothalamus. It is located at the base of the brain at the top of the brainstem. Underneath the hypothalamus and connected to it is a tiny gland called the pituitary, with a bulge at the front and another at the back. The hypothalamus acts either separately or together with the pituitary to both monitor and control at least six body functions and states.

The front of the hypothalamus works like a thermostat. It responds to nerve receptors in the skin that sense heat or cold. The hypothalamus signals the pituitary to release a chemical that triggers another gland to release thyroid hormone into the bloodstream. More of this hormone will cause the body to build up heat and begin sweating. Less will cause cooling or a cold feeling.

Other parts of the hypothalamus react to internal sensors that warn of too much salt in the blood, or perhaps of too little water in the body. These then cause the body to conserve water rather than eliminate it. Or they trigger feelings of thirst, so the body takes on additional water.

Another region acts as an "appestat" to regulate the body's eating habits. Normally a balance is achieved between undereating and overeating, keeping the body well supplied with nutrients.

Still another part of the hypothalamus controls the sex drive in both males and females. This in turn may be triggered by senses such as sight or smell or by thought patterns within the brain's cerebral cortex.

There is even a part of the hypothalamus involved in regulating aggression. This causes a person to take active steps for control of the environment or to meet some outside threat.

Actually neurons in the hypothalamus secrete as many as six separate hormones into the anterior, or front, lobe of the pituitary, sometimes called the master gland. This stimulates the pituitary to release hormones into the bloodstream which carries them throughout the body. However, the chemical messengers are coded so that only particular glands or cells are stimulated by each hormone. ACTH stimulates the adrenal glands. GH stimulates general body growth. TSH stimulates the thyroid gland. PRL stimulates female breasts to produce milk. And LH affects the sex glands, while FSH stimulates male testes to produce sperm or female ovaries to produce eggs. Certain of these organs act as glands in turn to produce their own specialized hormones. The adrenal glands produce norepinephrine and special steroids, the thyroid gland produces thyroxine to regulate metabolism, the testes produce the male sex hormone testosterone, and the ovaries produce estrogens and progesterone. All of these glands that secrete substances directly into the bloodstream to regulate other organs are called endocrine, meaning "to secrete within." And this network of glandular functions is called the endocrine system.

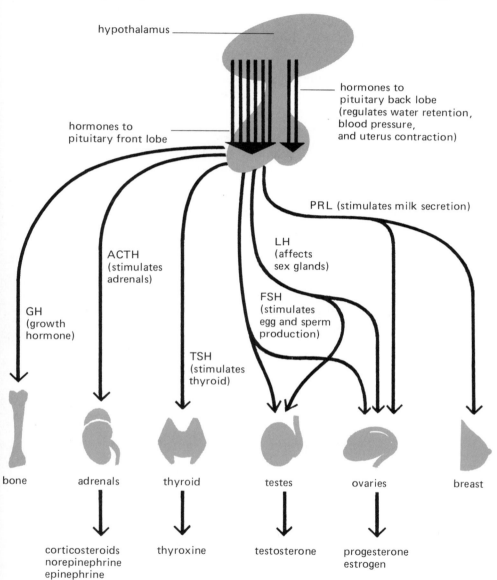

The endocrine system. Neurons in the hypothalamus secrete up to six hormones into the front lobe of the pituitary gland. The pituitary is triggered to release specialized hormones into the bloodstream that go to target glands and cells throughout the body. These in turn secrete still other hormones to regulate internal body functions.

The pituitary gland is indirectly linked to other important glands throughout the body. All of these respond to subtle amounts of chemical hormones released into the bloodstream. For an example, suppose a person must act quickly in a life-and-death situation such as a fire or an automobile accident. The hypothalamus signals the pituitary to secrete ACTH into the bloodstream. ACTH reaches the two adrenal glands, located on the top of each kidney, stimulating them to secrete extra amounts of epinephrine and norepinephrine. The blood carries these to certain organs, which then get ready to deal with the emergency.

Many parts of the brain seem to be involved in the common human emotions of love, joy, anger, pleasure, hatred, and others. Some of these are parts of the limbic system. For example, the small, nut-shaped amygdala is involved in expressions of rage. In an animal, if the amygdala is stimulated electrically, that animal will try to attack another animal. Or in humans, if the amygdala is removed through accident or surgery, the personality becomes more inhibited and childlike. Nerve cells in the reticular system, a network controlling wakefulness and the routing of signals, seem involved in other emotions. When too little norepinephrine is secreted, a person may feel depressed. On the other hand, when too much norepinephrine is produced, a person may have the anxiety and other emotions that accompany stress. And there is evidence that the secretion of the neurotransmitter dopamine may induce feelings of pleasure.

Various sections of the cerebral cortex also may be involved with emotional states and their control. In particular, the frontal cortex receives direct nerve connections from the thalamus. Thus the midbrain and forebrain are linked in complex combinations of thoughts and the feelings that accompany them.

The importance of the frontal lobes in emotion was pointed up by an accident that happened in 1848 to a twenty-five-year-old railroad worker named Phineas Gage. This capable young man was the foreman of a work crew that used explosives to clear a level roadbed. There was an accidental explosion. A crowbar was blown upward like an oversized bullet through Gage's head, entering below the cheek and exiting above the forehead. This freak accident damaged the left frontal lobe of his brain. Amazingly, Gage lived and recovered, but he underwent a drastic personality change through the loss of his left frontal lobe. He became unable to control his temper. He got into violent arguments and even fights at the slightest provocation. At times he behaved more like an animal than like a human. This unusual accident was one of the first cases to show how important the frontal lobes are in regulating emotional balance.

Recent studies of electrical activity in the frontal regions suggest that areas of the left side of the brain actually control positive emotions such as happiness and joy, while parts of the right side may be more involved in negative emotions such as sadness and disgust.

Drugs

The brain is in a constantly changing state. It swings from hyperactivity through normal and resting states to sleep and even unconsciousness. All of these states are associated with chemical changes in the brain. These changes also can be induced by chemicals from outside the body. Such chemicals may be a part of the food we eat. Or they may be the natural and synthetic chemicals used as medications or for other purposes. These substances are the drugs, and they range from chemicals that are beneficial to those that can be addictive or destructive and can even bring death if misused.

For convenience, drugs affecting the nervous system can be divided into five groups: sedatives, painkillers, tranquilizers, stimulants, and hallucinogens. The groups overlap, but these five categories are useful ones.

Sedatives, also called depressants, depress the level of consciousness or alertness and induce sleep. Barbiturates, such as amytal or phenobarbital, act on the reticular system to cause drowsiness. They are commonly used as sleeping pills. Unfortunately, they are habit-forming. If taken too regularly, the body may come to depend on them. Stopping their use then can bring illness or even convulsions.

A common depressant is alcohol. It decreases electrical activity in the hippocampus and depresses the central nervous system, starting with the higher brain centers. A person taking alcohol first loses judgment, then becomes less inhibited as the lower brain centers take over. This makes the person moody and emotional. Gradually, more and more of the brain's control centers are depressed. Speech is slurred, and body movements are uncoordinated. Alcohol also can be addictive, permanently affecting behavior and causing damage to body organs such as the kidneys and liver, as well as to the brain.

The most common painkiller is aspirin, which originates as a natural substance found in the bark of the willow tree. This drug appears to act on pain centers in the thalamus. Other chemicals with painkilling qualities are used as local or general anesthetics. Chloroform, nitrous oxide, novocaine, xylocaine, and other agents act by preventing nerves from conducting signals. These may be local nerves or more extensive parts of the nervous system or brainstem. Thus normal pain signals do not reach the brain. Or the level of conscious awareness may be reduced enough so that pain is not noticed. This can happen when a general anesthetic is used for a major operation.

An important group of painkillers is the opiates. These chemicals originate from the seed head of the opium poppy flower. Heroin, morphine, methadone, codeine, and Demerol are all opiates. Nerve fibers from the body's pain receptors connect in the spinal column to fibers leading to the brain. A natural chemical called substance P is involved in transmitting these pain signals.

Fortunately, the body also makes its own painkillers. They are called endorphins, which means "morphine from within." Both opiates and endorphins latch onto special receptor sites on the surface of nerve cells. The nerves then fire their pain signals less often, or not at all. Such receptor sites can also be found in the limbic system. Thus the opiates not only are powerful painkillers but can counteract depression and induce a sense of euphoria. This feeling of a "high" is what abusers of these drugs seek. Regular use of opiates is addictive, and it takes larger and larger amounts to get the desired high. A decrease in the amount of opiates in the body then results in depression, chills, and tremors. Such addiction is severe and very difficult to treat.

Tranquilizers exert a calming effect without depressing alertness. They act on the hypothalamus and the limbic system. These drugs include such trade names as Librium, Valium, and Miltown. They are helpful in reducing the anxiety and panic often present in emotional disturbances. Other chemicals called psychotherapeutic agents may be effective in controlling the symptoms of schizophrenia, a group of diseases known to particularly affect young adults, in which they feel alienated, harassed, and confused. In such cases chlorpromazine, a psychotherapeutic agent, also acts on the natural neurotransmitter called dopamine, reducing amounts present in the brain and relieving the disturbing symptoms.

Stimulants have an effect opposite to that of sedatives, tranquilizers, psychotherapeutic agents, and painkillers. Stimulants multiply the effect of the natural brain chemical norepinephrine. This is the transmitter of the sympathetic nervous system that helps prepare the body for emergencies. Typical stimulants are the caffeine found in coffee, tea, and some soft drinks; the nicotine found in ordinary cigarettes; and cocaine. Amphetamines, sometimes called pep pills or uppers, also release the norepinephrine stored in the brain. Athletes sometimes take amphetamines to stimulate performance. Others take them to avoid sleep in order to continue studying or working. However, these short-term advantages often are outweighed by adverse effects. These can include headaches, dry mouth, palpitations of the heart, sweating, nervousness, and even depression leading to symptoms that resemble those of schizophrenia.

Hallucinogens are drugs that distort the senses and trigger illusions. They include mescaline and LSD, which is short for the very long chemical term lysergic acid diethylamide, sometimes called simply "acid." Most drugs of this type stimulate the sympathetic nervous system. This raises blood pressure, increases heart rate, and causes sweating. Sensory pathways become overloaded, any or all of the senses may seem magnified or more acute, and emotions are heightened. At the same time judgment and memory are suppressed. Sensory illusions can take the form of brilliant light, fantastic scenes, or odd mixtures of sounds and sights. A person may feel invincible, as if he or she can fly, and personality becomes more childlike. Hallucinogens are sometimes used to treat psychological illness. But when taken only for a "high" they can cause drastic mood swings and uncontrolled behavior, even including suicide.

Perhaps the most common drug in this broad group is marijuana, which comes from the cannabis plant. The smoke inhaled from burning plant parts affects the brain and body. Marijuana actually abolishes the reflexes of the sympathetic nervous system. It lowers body temperature and increases appetite but reduces stomach acid and may cause vomiting. Once thought to be a relatively harmless hallucinogen, it has been found to destroy brain cells, which cannot be replaced. Marijuana is most harmful to children and teenagers, who are still developing.

Thus drugs have led researchers to important discoveries about the chemistry of the brain and its control. They have been used successfully to treat various illnesses. At the same time, their unprescribed use in regular and large amounts has become a dramatic social problem, damaging the brains and personalities of thousands of victims.

Sleep and Waking

The human body has its own natural rhythms. For example, each person has a twenty-four-hour temperature cycle. During the day there is a slight, gradual rise in body temperature with a peak sometime during the afternoon. This time will vary from person to person, but for each individual it usually is quite consistent. In the evening body temperature falls, reaching its lowest toward the end of the night. At the same time there is a shorter cycle of attention and relaxation that occurs about every ninety minutes during the day. This pattern is subtle during waking hours, but at night, during sleep, the same ninety-minute cycle controls a remarkable series of changes in the brain and body that repeats throughout the night.

Within the brainstem is a tangled mass of neurons called the reticular formation. A part of this is the reticular activating system, or RAS. This system plays an important part in wakefulness. From this same part of the brainstem or midbrain small structures called the raphe nuclei and the locus coeruleus, whose name means "blue place," send nerve fibers downward to targets in the spinal cord, backward to the cerebellum, and upward to the thalamus. The raphe nuclei transfer a chemical called serotonin. The locus coeruleus nerve fibers transfer norepinephrine. These two chemicals are very important in setting the state of activity or depression of the brain.

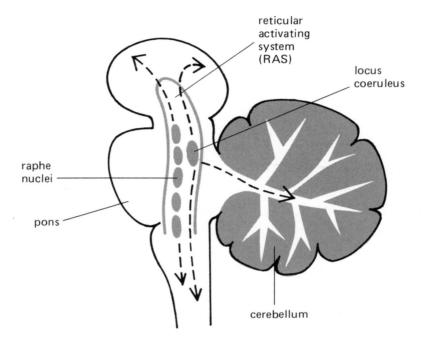

Simplified schematic of brain parts that regulate sleep and waking. Dotted arrows show neurotransmitter paths.

During wakefulness the RAS joins with incoming signals to turn the cortex "on" and stimulate the brain and body to action. But during sleep these "on" signals to higher brain centers are normally decreased.

Once activity has been blocked, sleep begins. Each ninety-minute cycle of sleep consists of stages or brain states that can be monitored with a special machine called an electroencephalograph, or EEG. The name means "electric head writing." And the electrical signals that are recorded by the machine come from the brain itself. Electrical wires, or electrodes, can be pasted on the skull. Groups of brain cells fire in patterns that produce small changes in electrical voltage. These changes can be detected by the electrodes at the surface of the scalp. The electrical patterns are converted into vibrations, which are electronically recorded onto paper.

Normally when a person is awake the pattern is one of rapid and irregular spikes that have no particular rhythm. These are called beta waves, from one letter of the Greek alphabet. However, just before a person falls asleep, the pattern changes to one of more regular vibrations that occur between eight and twelve times per second. On the chart this pattern looks quite different from the wakeful beta pattern and marks the first stage of sleep. It has been given the name alpha waves.

As real sleep begins, the wave patterns slow in frequency to from three to seven pulses per second. These are called theta waves and are typical of this second stage of sleep. As sleep deepens into a third stage, there are bursts of spikes and spindles that interrupt the theta waves. Then, in stage four, the waves become more regular again and even slower in frequency, from only about one-half to two pulses per second. These are delta waves, and this is the deepest stage of sleep.

The fifth stage is a mysterious mixture of mental states and bodily activity. It is so peculiar that it has been called paradoxical sleep. This is the sleep in which dreams occur. Eyelids twitch, the body may jerk, and in males the penis almost always becomes erect. Yet, at the same time, the neck and skeletal muscles are completely relaxed, almost as if the body were paralyzed. The twitches in the closed eyelids are because the eyeballs are moving beneath them, just as they do when awake. These twitches are called rapid eye movements, or REM, and can be measured by electrodes pasted at the outer corners of the eyes. The electrical charges from muscle movements of the eyes are registered as broad swinging lines on the chart paper of the EEG machine. If a person is awakened during this stage, he or she will report a dream.

It has been found that just before REM sleep begins, a small part of the brainstem, the pons, suddenly increases the rate at which its neurons fire. This stops when REM sleep is complete. At the same time, the chemical signals from the raphe nuclei and locus coeruleus stop completely during REM sleep.

In this unusual stage of dream sleep it is as if the mind has been aroused from deep sleep and returned to wakefulness. But the signals connecting the brain and the body are blocked so that sleep is preserved. Then after the REM stage is complete, the sleeper will return to stage two and begin another ninety-minute cycle. Each time the cycle repeats, sleep is less deep, so that by the end of the night the deeper sleep stages may be skipped entirely. At the same time, the periods of dream sleep become longer through the night. The first dream may last only about fifteen minutes, but the last dream of the night may last as long as forty-five minutes. This is why you will sometimes awaken in the morning before finishing the last dream, and you may easily remember what that dream was about.

Even a fetus in its mother's uterus has rapid eye movements. Ultrasound waves that are too high in frequency for the human ear to detect can safely penetrate living tissue. They are reflected like radar to reveal the shape of more dense structures within the body. Ultrasound signals can show the shape of the unborn baby

Below: Brain-wave patterns of waking, resting and sleeping. Alpha waves indicate a relaxed state. Theta waves are associated with creative imagery, and delta waves with deep sleep. Rapid eye movements occur during dreams.

waking   stage 1   stage 2
beta waves   alpha waves   theta waves

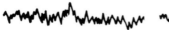  

with details of the facial features. Even the flickering of the closed eyelids, which is characteristic of REM sleep, can be seen. So apparently from before the time of birth, all humans begin the patterns of rapid eye movements associated with dreams.

Researchers do not agree on the function of dreams. It is clear that the pons sends signals to the rest of the brain just as if sensory cues were coming from outside the body. The fact is that outer sensory signals are blocked from reaching the brain during sleep. But the brain treats the signals from the pons as if they were real. This may be why some dreams seem to be a jumble of nonsense. Therefore, one possible function of dreams may be simply to scan the daily collection of brain impressions and discard those no longer needed.

Some sensory clues do leak into inner awareness, however. Suppose you are asleep in a cold room and the blankets slide off. Instead of waking up, you might have a dream that you are walking outside in a winter storm without a coat. Or the sound of a fly buzzing around in the bedroom might trigger a dream about a lawn mower or a motorboat. Clearly, your brain and mind act as storytellers to make sense of both the world outside you and the inner world of thoughts and memories.

Dreams can be a blend of memories of recent events and of events that you have consciously forgotten but are stored nevertheless. Clinicians have learned through the use of hypnosis, which is simply an unusually concentrated focus of attention, that even memories of early childhood can be recalled in great detail at certain times. And all such memories are part of the material out of which dreams are built.

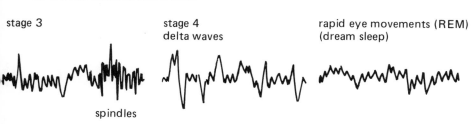

stage 3

stage 4
delta waves

rapid eye movements (REM)
(dream sleep)

spindles

Experimenters have found that we all dream regularly throughout prolonged sleep. If we are not allowed to dream, we become extremely irritable and less able to function when we are awake. It seems that dreaming regularly helps us to cope with our lives and our problems in a practical and creative way that keeps us mentally in balance.

The study of dreams has brought new discoveries and questions about the nature of mind and consciousness. For example, one type of exceptionally clear dream is called lucid. It is almost as if the dreamer is wide awake. A lucid dream occasionally is of a distant place or event, as if the dreamer actually is there at the scene. Perhaps the dreamer "sees" an airplane crash in a faraway locale. The next day the newspaper has a photograph of the crashed plane, verifying certain details of the lucid dream as they had appeared earlier to the dreamer. This ability of the mind to "travel" away from the brain and body, or even forward or backward in time, suggests that conscious awareness is not just the total activity of the brain, but rather a form of independent energy that uses the brain as a tool. Such questions are among the unsolved puzzles of mind and its capabilities.

5

MEMORY, THOUGHT, AND THERAPY

Learning and Memory

Learning and memory are complicated brain functions being studied by many investigators. Certain chemicals such as dopamine, acetylcholine, and norepinephrine seem to stimulate brain activity that results in memory and learning. And throughout the brain and nervous system the groups of complex molecules called proteins constantly are being broken down and replaced. Experiments show that when learning takes place, proteins build up. Apparently, such proteins may travel along a neuron to the synapse, perhaps changing it in ways that make it more effective for a time.

While neurons do not reproduce themselves and even die over a period of years, they nevertheless grow thicker networks of extensions. Tiny trial fibers actually are sent out in search of new contacts. Some networks are built, then discarded. Others continue to increase throughout life. Thus learning involves both building up new nerve connections and eliminating other ones.

The brain is a very flexible tool. If one part is damaged, another will begin to take over its functions. For instance, in a

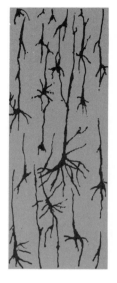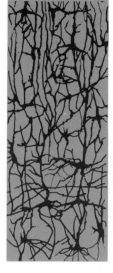

At 15 months of age a growing child has more nerve extensions and contacts than at 3 months of age. Some extensions will be discarded. Others will increase throughout life.

3 months   15 months

disease called hydrocephalus pressure from fluid inside the skull increases, and so brain parts are compressed to a fraction of normal size. Usually intelligence is dulled. Nevertheless, in a few cases all the important brain functions apparently can be carried out by the remaining tissue. The afflicted person may then be of normal intelligence, or occasionally above average.

The cortex of the brain consists of many layers of cells. These cells are interconnected in vertical columns with perhaps 100 neurons in each column. The higher mental activities of thought and association involve electrical and chemical changes within these columns and between groups of columns. These changes may take the form of feedback loops involving a few cells or complex overall patterns of chemical codes and may be temporary or permanent.

Some types of learning depend on repeated use of the visual and spatial centers found mostly in the brain's right hemisphere. Others depend on an ability to use language, usually associated with the brain's left hemisphere. In this sense, we truly think with the words we know and the ways in which they can be linked together.

Memory and learning are interdependent. In order to learn, the brain must retain information so that it can be compared and analyzed. Memory is of several basic kinds. The first kind is short-term memory. This is the ability to retain for a short time names or numbers, up to about seven units, by concentrating on them and repeating them. A local telephone number, such as 395-1815, and an automobile license plate combining numbers and letters are good examples. Such a unit may be remembered for only a short time, say, as long as it takes to look up the phone number and dial it—or as long as it takes for a police officer to memorize the license number of a suspicious car before jotting it down.

Long-term memory is more permanent and usually involves material that is used again and again. If names and phone numbers are those of good friends, they are reinforced by constant use and so become a part of long-term memory.

A third basic type of memory is called eidetic, meaning "of a form." This type is also called photographic memory. Somehow the eye and brain register all the details of a scene, or perhaps all the words on the page of a book. Later the person can describe the scene as if looking at a photograph or can perfectly visualize the book page and all the words on it. Eidetic memory is more common in children, although some people keep the ability throughout life.

Memory skills vary between the hemispheres of the brain. The left brain may recall isolated details and verbal units, such as the spelling of names. The right brain remembers shapes, spaces, and overall patterns, such as musical melodies or the contours of familiar faces.

It has been found that the hippocampus, in the center of the brain, is of primary importance in learning and memory. Apparently incoming signals are processed there, grouped, and retained briefly before being routed to sections of the cortex. A person with severe damage to the hippocampus will keep the ability to recall previously learned material but lose the ability to process and store new information.

The ability to learn and remember new material may decrease with age. The reasons are not entirely clear. However, a Swedish researcher named Anders Bjorklund carried out a surprising experiment. He removed brain cells from the hippocampus of a young rat and implanted them into the hippocampus of an old rat. The old rat then was able to learn new tasks much better than before.

In practice most memory depends on association. The process is simple. Let's say you are going to the grocery store to buy bananas, corn flakes, eggs, cheese, a sponge, and a bottle of diet soda. The idea is to create a story in which all these objects are related. The more fantastic the story, the easier it will be to remember the connections. Suppose a bunch of bananas all have arms and legs and are holding arms dancing around in a circle. They look really "flaky." So imagine corn flakes stuck all over them. In the middle of the circle is a stack of eggs, and the dancing bananas have to be careful not to step on the eggs and break them. Someone is pouring melted cheese all over the eggs, creating a sticky mess. It looks so terrible that you have to get a wet sponge to clean it up. This is such hard work that you get tired and thirsty, and you decide to relax by having a cool drink of diet cola.

The story is so silly that you cannot easily forget it. So in remembering the story you automatically remember its parts, which, of course, are the items in the list. In fact, without being aware of it, you have already made many such association links to remember all the things you now know.

The ancient Greeks taught an association system to help students remember a long speech. The idea was to choose a well-known building with many separate parts. The student could set up a tour of the building, going from one section to another in a logical way. Once the route was learned, a speech could be remembered by picturing the important ideas in proper order in the various rooms. It worked the same way as the story about the shopping list, except that in this case the various rooms would link the story together. The student would travel mentally through the rooms and would automatically "see" the entire speech before his eyes.

Some people have very unusual memory abilities. One famous case comes from neurologist A. R. Luria, who tested a Russian newspaper reporter named Solomon-Veniaminovich Shereshevski. Shereshevski claimed to be able to remember everything he saw or did in perfect detail. He even had trouble trying to forget things that were not important. Luria investigated Shereshevski over a long period. He set up difficult lists and tables of numbers and other items for the reporter to memorize. Shereshevski could remember them all even years later, along with details of what was going on around him at the time of each test.

It turned out that the newspaper reporter was using basic association but in a very elaborate way. He made up stories with rhymes and puns using fences, buildings, roads, and other familiar places. He did this automatically, as if it were the most natural thing in the world.

Shereshevski also had a peculiar memory abnormality called synesthesia. Sounds made him think of colors and textures. For instance, he might sense one sound as being "blue and rough," while another was "orange and smooth." Shereshevski also had more trouble remembering faces than the average person. But these problems were separate from his remarkable ability to memorize detailed lists and tables.

An exciting theory of human memory has come from neuropsychologist Karl Pribram. This theory compares memory with a hologram. A hologram is a three-dimensional photograph made with laser light of exceptionally pure color and direction. To create the image, a laser light beam is projected toward an object. The light is reflected from the object to the surface of a film. This beam of light is called the information beam. At the same time, part of the original laser beam is split off with a special mirror. This unaltered beam also strikes the surface of the film. There the original beam and the information beam intersect to make what is called an interference pattern at the film's surface. No visible image appears on the developed film as in an ordinary photograph.

However, when a laser beam of the same color or frequency as the original light passes through the film, the observer sees a solid image of the photographed object. It seems to hang in midspace behind the film, or sometimes even in front of it! The observer can move around somewhat to get different views of the object as if looking through a window. The object looks real and solid from every angle.

In a hologram every part of the film carries information about the whole image. The film can be cut up into small sections. The same laser light directed through any piece of the film will produce an image of the complete object. The image will not be as clear and bright as that produced with a larger piece of film, but the shape of the object will be complete. The word for this unusual property of a hologram is *redundant,* which means "happening again."

Memory storage in the human brain also seems redundant. That is, memories seem to be stored in many parts of the brain at once. Sometimes even a large part of the brain may be destroyed, yet particular memories can still be complete. A brain process that works like the storage of information in a hologram may be part of the answer to this puzzle. For example, when even a single nerve cell fires in the brain, the electrical pulse travels out along the axons of that cell. Nerve cells receiving this information pulse pass it along to distribute it more widely. Such a pulse with many small elements all moving along together is called a wave front. Already that pulse is redundant because it is in many places at once.

Suppose that another wave front of nerve pulses comes from elsewhere in the brain and overlaps with the first wave front. This is the sort of thing that happens if you drop two pebbles into a pond at the same time some distance apart. Circular ripples spread out around the spot where each pebble struck the water. Eventually they overlap. The intersections form a new pattern that gives information about each of the original wave fronts. In just this way the intersections of electrical wave fronts in the brain create patterns spread across many nerve cells, and each pattern may be stored as coded chemical information.

Many holograms can be stored on the same film at the same time. Each one can be decoded separately by the same laser light that created it. It is only necessary to choose different pure colors or frequencies of light so that the spacing of the wave pulses is different for each hologram contained on the same film.

In the same way, perhaps, the brain might "tune in" to the frequency of only one coded message at a time, and an almost

Pebbles dropped in a pond create waves that intersect to form new patterns. Nerve signals in the brain also generate wavefronts that intersect. One memory theory suggests that overlapping intersections may permit holographic storage of information.

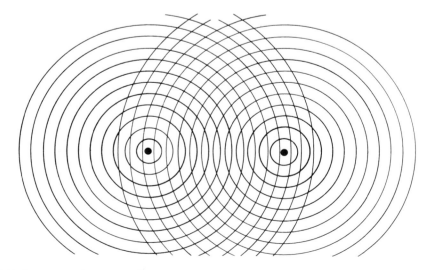

endless number of messages could overlap throughout the brain. In fact, because the protein molecules of the brain are so tiny, the human brain easily could holographically store up to one quadrillion bits of information with no confusion. It is possible that in this way every single brain cell has some awareness of everything the brain "knows."

Mind Control

An exciting advance in the understanding of mental abilities and brain states has come through biofeedback. *Bio* means "life," and feedback means information about the living body returned to itself. The feedback information is about body functions that normally are unconscious or automatic. A good example is control of blood flow and body temperature.

In one biofeedback experiment a temperature sensor was designed to be attached to the fingertip of a volunteer. By watching the needle on a temperature dial, the volunteer could see when the hand was warmer than usual. And through remembering the feeling, he or she could practice warming the hand just by thinking about it.

A woman who often had migraine headaches was participating in the experiment. During one training session she felt a headache coming on. At the same time, she was getting a tingling feeling in her hands, and the needle showed they were warmer. To her surprise, this change caused the headache to go away. Soon she learned to warm her hands at particular times in order to avoid oncoming headaches. She would sit calmly in a chair and think to herself, "Blood, go down." The headache came from too much blood flow to the head. The increase of blood to the hands caused a decrease in the head, which relieved the headache.

In the same way biofeedback can be used to achieve a particular brain state. For example, a person's brain waves can be fed through electrodes to equipment that changes the pulses to sounds. One can learn to identify his or her own brain waves by listening to the sounds. When the sounds come smoothly at about ten pulses per second, the brain is generating alpha waves. Or when the pulses slow to about five per second, theta waves are being produced. Alpha and theta frequencies go with relaxed states that help reduce stress and develop creative imagination. One uses biofeedback to recognize the states and then learns to duplicate them at will. Actually the brain and nervous system are constantly using internal feedback to monitor body states, movements, positions, and chemical balance. The new biofeedback methods simply bring the same process to the level of wakeful consciousness.

Meditation and hypnosis accomplish similar changes in mind and body states. In meditation one quietly concentrates on a single sound by repeating it mentally over and over. Or one concentrates on slow and regular breathing. The mind is cleared of conflicting thoughts, and a relaxed and beneficial state is attained. Heartbeat is slower, blood sugar is reduced, and there is a feeling of calm energy.

With hypnosis there is a strong focus of attention in one direction, like being caught up in watching a good movie. Another person can suggest what to focus on—an idea, an image, or a memory. Or a person can use self-hypnosis by choosing a mental idea and repeating it until the mind and body act as if that is the most important thing.

Any of these techniques can bring about remarkable changes in brain and body chemistry and balance. An athlete can imagine a goal in advance in order to perform better. An overexcited person can be calmed. Pain can be reduced. In fact, through hypnosis some people can experience such complete loss of pain that an operation can be performed without anesthesia. Hypnosis using stereo headphones with music, narration, or noise has proved effective in blocking pain in dentistry, for example.

Treatment

Many different kinds of professionals work with problems of the brain and mind. Psychiatrists, psychologists, and counselors primarily study and work with mind and mood in an effort to understand human behavior and emotional problems. A psychiatrist is trained in both medicine and psychology and can prescribe medications to change brain chemistry for the better.

Neurobiologists and brain specialists, on the other hand, are concerned mainly with the physical aspects of the brain, its functions, and how it can be treated through chemistry and, at times, through surgery.

There are many ways to diagnose and treat problems of the brain and mind. One approach is chemical treatment. For instance, tests can be made to discover the levels of chemicals and traces of minerals in the brain. A hyperactive person might have too little zinc, a problem that can be corrected through nutrition and diet. Someone with Parkinson's disease, in which there are uncontrolled nerve impulses and muscle movements, may have too little dopamine in the brain. Taking the drug L-dopa can balance the brain and make body movements more normal. Or a schizophrenic may actually have too much natural dopamine and a blocking chemical can be prescribed. Besides the usual means of administering chemicals, a mechanical device has been developed that can be worn outside the body to periodically inject certain chemicals into the brain to replace those missing because of accidental brain damage or chemical imbalance.

Today there are clever techniques for viewing the living brain. For example, a narrow device called an endoscope can be slid into the area between the skull and the brain. This instrument carries a miniature light and lens system that magnifies the image to allow a physician to see the detail of a tiny inside area. The brain itself has no pain receptors, so devices and probes of this kind cause little discomfort. And because they are narrow, they cause almost no initial tissue damage.

There are several other ways to view the living brain and to learn about brain activity—how it reacts to certain drugs, for instance. One of these techniques is the CAT scan. The letters stand for "computerized axial tomography." Through a doughnut-shaped device placed around the head a series of X-ray images is made from various points on the circle, all passing through the same cross section of the head. A computer analyzes the combined density readings, and a picture emerges of that part of the head and brain.

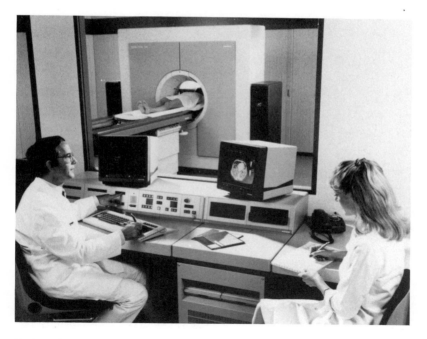

Patient is placed in position for CAT scan. X-ray paths are analyzed by computer. Reconstructed cross sections of body and spinal column or head and brain are projected on video screen.

A second type of brain scan is called nuclear magnetic resonance imaging, or NMR. Like the CAT scan, this shows a structural image, but the detail is clearer. With NMR the protons of the brain's atoms are stimulated to line up like tiny magnetic tops, all spinning and wobbling in the same direction. The energy released is like a radio broadcast from the brain's own cells. A computer collects this information and creates a picture of a cross section of the brain projected onto a screen.

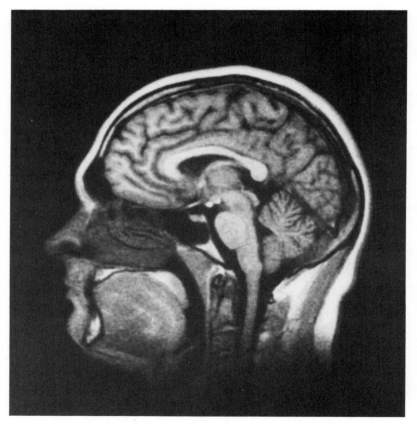

NMR scan showing vertical cross section of brain and brainstem with exceptional detail.

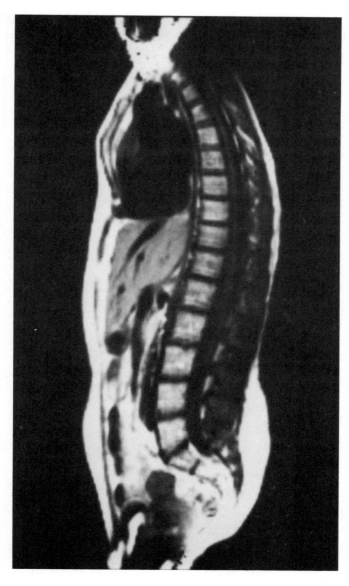

NMR scan showing vertical cross section of spinal column.

Another technique is the PET, or positron emission tomography, scan. Radioactive sugar is injected into the body. In the brain the radioactive material gives off positrons—positively charged atomic particles—that collide with the electrons of the brain cells. Radiation from the collisions is collected by detectors in the PET apparatus around the head. For a short time a TV-type picture shows the active chemical charges in the brain as glowing colors. The reds, blues, and yellows may expand and shift, showing normal activity or that of an unhealthy brain. For example, a patient listening to music might show brighter color and more activity in the right hemisphere of the brain. The activities of thinking and speaking will show other color highlights, particularly on the left side of the brain and the front.

In contrast, the PET scan of a patient with Alzheimer's disease, a disorder affecting increasing numbers of older people in which certain brain cells have become tangled and useless, will show the odd distribution at the back of the head that is typical of this illness. In fact, examination of tissue from the brains of Alzheimer's patients who have died now reveals the presence of virus-like organisms similar to those associated with several slow-developing brain disorders. Thus research into infectious diseases, combined with improved diagnosis through brain scans, may hasten the discovery of a vaccine or cure for Alzheimer's disease.

Although rarely necessary, in some cases scans and other tests will indicate the need for brain surgery. It may be as simple as implanting a very narrow hollow tube that can penetrate the brain's innermost cavities, or ventricles, to draw off fluid when there is too much pressure, as in hydrocephalus. Or it may be more extensive if a tumor is involved. Thanks to modern technology, brain surgery is now very refined and precise. Today a very small amount of brain tissue can be

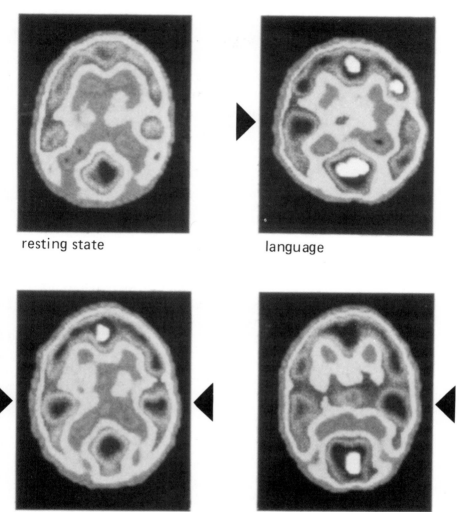

resting state   language

language and music   music

PET scans show horizontal sections of the living brain. In the resting state the ears are plugged. When listening to language alone there is bright activity on the left side of the brain. When listening to music alone there is activity on the right side. Listening to language and music together produces activity on both sides. Notice also the activity in frontal lobes (top) and visual centers (bottom) of each brain scan.

pinpointed and destroyed by using such tools as an electrical probe. Through a tiny opening in the skull the probe is easily inserted through brain tissue like a vaccination needle. A small electrical charge sent to the tip of the probe can first stimulate a response that lets the surgeon know that the correct point in the brain has been reached. Then a larger charge can destroy a small group of unwanted cells in that area. A technique called cryosurgery uses a similar probe to freeze and destroy small amounts of brain tissue without damage to surrounding areas. New techniques of laser surgery use a narrow focused beam of light in place of a probe to accomplish remarkably delicate surgery.

Another approach to therapy is through the emotions. A psychiatrist may privately discuss the meaning of a patient's dreams and feelings. Group therapy may be used in which members share experiences or act out the contents of their dreams for each other. Association techniques, such as those that are useful for memory and learning, may be used to explore deeply seated fears or other emotions. Or perhaps hypnosis may be used to recover suppressed memories of earlier events that are causing unsolved problems. A psychologist may perform various tests to determine patterns of anxiety or mental illness. Many times, a patient can best be treated by a combination of psychological help and prescribed medication.

6

FUTURE

Ongoing research is rapidly bringing both more answers and more questions about the remarkable workings of the human brain. It is important to each of us to learn how these developments may affect our lives in the future.

Because there are so many advanced techniques for observation, therapy, and surgery, the question is sometimes asked whether brain tissue can be transplanted. Experiments with organ transplants already prove that body parts such as kidneys or hearts can be successfully transplanted from one person to another. Animal tissues such as catgut, or intestines, have been used in human surgery for years. And an animal heart from a baboon has temporarily been transplanted into a human being. Although the problems of transplanting brain cell tissue are much greater, there is some possibility that this could be done in the future.

In one group of experiments, living cells from the adrenal glands of a rat were extracted and planted within a rat brain, where they then stimulated the production of missing hormones.

In other experiments, cells of the human adrenal medulla were transplanted into the caudate nucleus of human patients suffering from Parkinson's disease, the nervous disorder that affects motor control. These studies are tentative but suggest that this procedure may be as effective in humans as in animals.

In both Canada and Sweden experiments have been carried out in transplanting nerve tissue into the brain from elsewhere in the body. For example, incisions are first made in the brain of an animal under anesthetic. Then from an extremity of the body of the same animal a small section of the peripheral nervous system is surgically removed. The segment is inserted into the cut area of the animal brain. This stimulates central nervous system neurons in the brain to grow fiber extensions into the peripheral nerve tissue and then back into the brain again. At the same time, the transplanted tissue regenerates severed connections. The synapses between transplanted cells and host cells work just like normal connections. Thus the natural tendency of neurons to put out new branches may make it possible for transplanted tissue to be accepted as part of the basic nerve network to replace that which is missing or damaged.

If brain sections in humans become transplanted even on a small scale, a puzzling question arises. Will the personality and memories of the recipient change to those of the donor? Possibly to some extent. But it is also likely that the rebuilt brain of the future may simply accept the new grafts as improved tools for the use of the conscious mind. If brain function is improved, personality can be expressed more fully. The patient may perhaps then become more "himself" or "herself."

Another important area of research is genetic engineering. Several brain disorders appear to be inherited from generation to generation. One of these is Huntington's disease, named for the physician who discovered it. Those who are afflicted lose brain cells in the caudate nucleus and the basal ganglia deep within the brain. As a result, their body motions become sudden and twisted, and faces take on a grotesque appearance. As yet there is no cure but a key to the disorder has been discovered in the DNA of cell molecules.

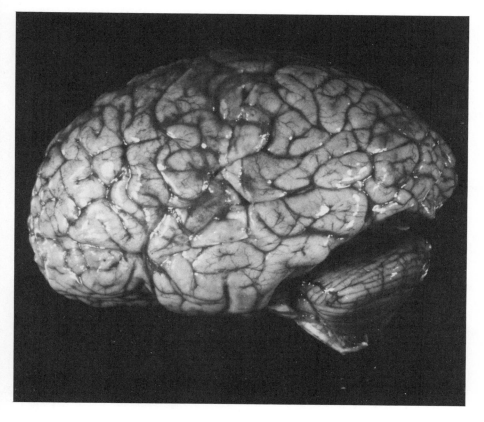

Actual photograph of human brain shown in side view. Frontal lobe is at left and cerebellum is at lower right. Note deep folds of the cortex.

The double strands of all DNA are made up of four base substances: adenine, thymine, cytosine, and guanine. These are called A, T, C, and G for short. The specific arrrangement of linked pairs of these substances along the twisted chromosomes of DNA is the information code of the genes. Researchers have found that people with Huntington's disease show a particular sequence of G's, C's, T's, and A's. Furthermore, if a section of the DNA strands called chromosome 4 is broken apart by enzymes, the pieces always have an identical length, thus marking those people who have Huntington's disease. Recently a similar genetic marker has been found in another chromosome among some patients with a mental illness called manic depression. This suggests that this disease, too, may be inherited.

By studying such DNA codes and markers, it may eventually be possible to introduce organisms into the brain to treat inherited diseases by altering genes directly. This is much like what happens when certain viruses invade the human body and borrow cellular material to reproduce themselves or to trigger the growth of foreign material. For instance, such viruslike cells have been found in the brains of patients who died from Alzheimer's disease. And just as an unwanted virus can invade and alter brain tissue, in a similar way a helpful brain virus might be introduced that could stimulate the correction of a genetic defect. Of course such procedures must be both scientifically safe and legally approved before being used on humans.

What about artificial intelligence? Will computers ever take over for brains? To some extent they already have. Designing computers is just one way the brain has of building "more" of itself. Whether it is a simple pocket calculator or the console used to track a space satellite, computers work as extensions of the human brain. Today such devices are manipulated outside the body. But there may be a time when miniature units could be placed within the skull to replace or supplement brain parts, perhaps even working on the low electrical voltages present in the brain itself.

Computers of today perform their functions very rapidly thanks to marvelous developments such as the transistor and to a microchip that can hold one million bits of information. Some of these microchips are already compatible in size with some of the neurons within the brain. Indeed, some silicon chips with neuronlike circuits are being called "silicrons." And using purely electrical signals, computers can function many times more rapidly than human neurons, which rely partly on chemical as well as electrical changes.

However, the speed with which the human brain can carry out complex comparisons and decisions on many levels at once still far outstrips the capabilities of computers. Scientists working on artificial intelligence, or AI, are starting to design equipment that carries out parallel functions instead of those only in a single series of steps. And they are exploring circuits that more closely resemble those of the brain's neurons. Much of the emphasis in AI has been on machines that handle language. Computers now scan the shapes of printed letters to "read" words. They store spellings and word definitions, and can begin to determine which of several definitions may be the correct one for each situation.

At Johns Hopkins University in Baltimore biophysicist Terry Sejnowski has developed an artificial intelligence computer that handles a basic 1000-word vocabulary and can pronounce the words correctly. The device uses 300 units simultaneously. These work somewhat like neurons in the brain, using some 10,000 connections, and are arranged in three "layers." The bottom layer handles input of alphabet letters. The middle layer detects letter combinations special to English, and the top layer generates speech sounds. There is no basic computer program. Instead, the machine is "taught" by introducing mathematical "rules" to correct mistakes. Thus there is a "training" process that moves in stages from babbling, to handling short words, to handling phrases, and then to making generalizations. Once these stages are complete, new vocabulary words can "read," and the machine can then pronounce the unfamiliar words correctly as long as these follow standard rules in English pronunciation. In this way, the computer is "learning to read," much as a child learns.

The basic challenge in AI is to develop machines that truly "think" as humans do. Such devices must handle both left brain functions such as counting and naming, and right brain functions such as pattern recognition and creative comparison at the same time. The computer must listen, speak, plan, test, and invent with the sensitivity of human consciousness. These are tall tasks for any machine, goals which may not be reached for some time to come.

Nevertheless, of all the creatures on earth, only humans have used their brains to build devices to imitate the brain's own abilities. It is this amazing ability of the human brain to understand, treat, and improve itself that promises an exciting future for the inventive human mind.

Glossary

AI—artificial intelligence

amygdala—"almond-shaped"; part of inner brain involved in emotion

autonomic nervous system—nerve network regulating inner organs and activities

axon—neuron extension that transmits electrochemical signals

basal ganglion—nerve bundle of inner brain that handles relay signals

biofeedback—feedback information about body states and functions normally unconscious or automatic

brainstem—short brain section directly above spinal cord

Broca's area—part of temporal lobe involved in speech, named for its discoverer

CAT—computerized axial tomography; sophisticated X-ray scanning technique

central nervous system—control unit consisting of the brain and spinal cord

cerebellum—"small brain"; primitive brain section at base of skull

cerebral cortex—"brain shell"; outer layer of cerebrum

cerebrum—most highly developed brain section, also called forebrain

cochlea—coiled, fluid-filled organ of the inner ear involved in sound sensations

DNA—deoxyribonucleic acid; protein material from which chromosome strands and genes are formed

dendrite—neuron extension that receives electrochemical signals

endorphin—neurotransmitter that suppresses pain signals

frontal lobe—front section of cortex involved in higher thought

hippocampus—"S"-shaped part of inner brain involved in memory and learning

hypothalamus—section of inner brain beneath thalamus, active in regulating body states

ion—atom that carries a positive or negative electrical charge

limbic system—compact brain section within inner "border" of cortex

medulla—widened section of brainstem

microtubule—narrow unit within a neuron that adds support and transfers chemicals

motor strip—section of cortex involved with motor commands

neuron—basic cell of nerve tissue; transmits and receives electrochemical signals

neurotransmitter—chemical exchanged at synapse

NMR—nuclear magnetic resonance; magnetic image scanning technique

norepinephrine—major neurotransmitter for the sympathetic nervous system

occipital lobe—rear section of cortex involved in vision

olfactory bulb—small brain organ involved in smell sensations

parietal lobe—section of cortex above and behind temporal lobe, involved in sensory response and muscle control

peripheral nervous system—nerve network connecting spinal column to body parts and extremities

PET—positron emission tomography; radioactive image scanning technique

pituitary gland—organ connected to hypothalamus that regulates body states and processes by releasing hormones into the bloodstream

pons—"bridge"; section of brainstem above medulla

RAS—reticular activating system; section of brainstem that regulates wakefulness and sleep

REM—rapid eye movement; activity of the eyeballs during dream sleep

synapse—minute gap separating one neuron from another

temporal lobe—side section of cortex involved in hearing and speech

thalamus—"inside chamber"; section of inner brain involved in organization and interactions

Wernicke's area—part of temporal lobe involved in language, named for its discoverer

Further Reading

Berger, Melvin. *Exploring the Mind and Brain.* New York: Crowell, 1983

The Diagram Group. *The Brain: A User's Manual.* New York: G.P. Putnam's Sons, 1982

Edwards, Betty. *Drawing on the Right Side of the Brain.* Los Angeles: J.P. Tarcher, 1979

Facklam, Margery & Howard. *The Brain: Magnificent Mind Machine.* New York: Harcourt, 1982

Hyde, Margaret O. *Artificial Intelligence* (A revision of *Computers That Think?*). Hillside, N.J.: Enslow Publishers, 1986

The Illustrated Encyclopedia of the Human Body. New York: Exeter Books, 1984

Kettelkamp, Larry. *Hypnosis: The Wakeful Sleep.* New York: William Morrow, 1975

Kettelkamp, Larry. *A Partnership of Mind and Body: Biofeedback.* New York: William Morrow, 1976

Kettelkamp, Larry. *Tricks of Eye and Mind: The Story of Optical Illusion.* New York: William Morrow, 1974

Kettelkamp, Larry. *Your Marvelous Mind.* Philadelphia: Westminster, 1980

Martin, Paul D. *Messengers to the Brain: Our Fantastic Five Senses.* Washington, D.C.: National Geographic Society, 1984

The Rand McNally Atlas of the Body and Mind. New York: Rand McNally, 1976

Sharp, Pat. *Brain Power: Secrets of a Winning Team.* New York: Lothrop, Lee & Shepard, 1984

Ward, Brian R. *The Brain and Nervous System.* New York: Franklin Watts, 1981

Index